FORESTS

JESS FRENCH

Illustrated by

ALEXANDER MOSTOV

IVY KIDS

CONTENTS

WHY *do* FORESTS MATTER?

Forests are crucial to life on Earth; without them our world would simply not be able to function. From beautiful gingkos to towering giant sequoias, there are over 60,000 different types of tree. They cover almost a third of the Earth's surface, and some of them have been around for thousands of years.

Trees are hugely important parts of the landscapes they live in, providing shelter, food and safety for around two-thirds of the world's animals. One forest alone – the Amazon rainforest in South America – is home to ten percent of the world's known species. Trees even provide the oxygen we breathe!

Yet all over the world, we are losing trees at a worrying rate. Sometimes, there are good reasons why trees are cut down, but often there are better ways of doing things, which take into account the needs of people, animals AND trees. Luckily, it is still within our power to change things.

In this book, you can find out more about the reasons trees are being cut down, and the effects of forest loss on people, animals and the planet. Then you can learn about the clever things scientists, farmers, conservationists and other people around the world are doing to help – and discover how YOU can make a difference too! Together, we can make sure that our forests are still around to be enjoyed for thousands more years to come.

FORESTS of the WORLD

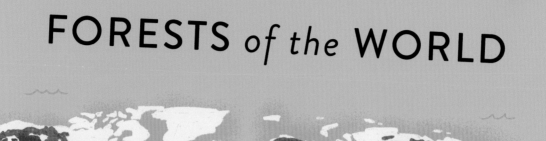

This map shows the forests of the world. You can find out more about taiga, temperate and tropical forests in the 'Earth's Forests' chapter.

■ **TAIGA FOREST**

■ **TEMPERATE FOREST**

■ **TROPICAL FOREST**

CHAPTER ONE
EARTH'S FORESTS

LARGE AREAS THAT ARE COVERED WITH TREES ARE KNOWN AS FORESTS. Some forests are hot and steamy, teeming with brightly coloured animals and clouds of insects, while others are cold and barren, with frozen rivers and tree branches drooping under the weight of heavy snow. It is this uniqueness that makes forests so special. No two forests are alike and, because of this, every forest is important. Sadly, there is one thing that all forests have in common – they are all threatened by deforestation.

TROPICAL RAINFORESTS

Inside a tropical rainforest, it is dark and steamy. The towering trees block out most of the light, and rain falls most days. Everywhere you look there are signs of life – lush, dense greenery fills every spare centimetre and the air throbs with the sounds of insects and birds. Around half of all the Earth's plants and animals live in these unique habitats. Scientists have identified four main layers inside all rainforests. Each is home to different animals and plants.

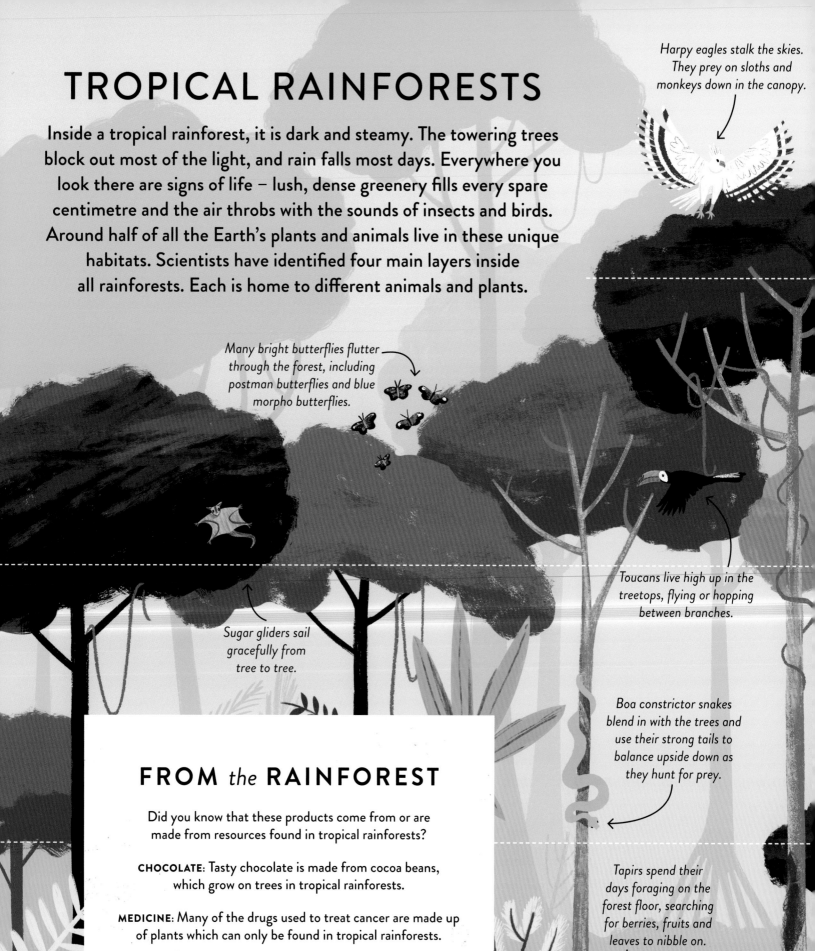

Harpy eagles stalk the skies. They prey on sloths and monkeys down in the canopy.

Many bright butterflies flutter through the forest, including postman butterflies and blue morpho butterflies.

Toucans live high up in the treetops, flying or hopping between branches.

Sugar gliders sail gracefully from tree to tree.

Boa constrictor snakes blend in with the trees and use their strong tails to balance upside down as they hunt for prey.

Tapirs spend their days foraging on the forest floor, searching for berries, fruits and leaves to nibble on.

FROM *the* RAINFOREST

Did you know that these products come from or are made from resources found in tropical rainforest?

CHOCOLATE: Tasty chocolate is made from cocoa beans, which grow on trees in tropical rainforests.

MEDICINE: Many of the drugs used to treat cancer are made up of plants which can only be found in tropical rainforests.

FRUIT: Delicious fruits like mangoes, bananas and avocados all grow in tropical rainforests.

Fast-growing Kapok trees like this one can reach heights of up to 70m.

Slow-moving sloths hang, perfectly camouflaged. Their long claws help them hold on to branches.

EMERGENT LAYER
In the top layer of the rainforest, the tallest trees, called emergents, get the most light.

CANOPY LAYER
The plants here receive plenty of rainwater and light. Most of the rainforest's animals live in this layer, feeding on the abundant fruit, leaves and flowers.

Spotted jaguars spend much of their time in this layer. The dappled, shadowy darkness of the understory makes it easy for them to slink unseen and pounce on prey.

Howler monkeys call out from the canopy, while squirrel monkeys hang out in the understory.

Indigenous peoples rely on the forest for everything they need to survive, including food, medicines and shelter. Sometimes they clear small areas to grow crops.

UNDERSTORY LAYER
In this dark and gloomy layer, shorter trees battle for sunlight.

Huge tree roots called buttresses spread out, supporting the massive trunks.

FOREST FLOOR LAYER
Only 1 percent of the sunlight reaches down here. Dead leaves fall to the ground where they decompose quickly, making the surface soil rich with nutrients.

TAIGA FORESTS

These ghostly forests cover more of the planet than any other. The days here can be long, snowy and hard. Summers are short, and the freezing winters stretch on for up to nine months at a time. Despite the harsh conditions, life thrives here! The land is packed with evergreens – trees that keep their leaves throughout the year – and the forest is full of swamps, lakes and rivers. These features attract and shelter many fascinating creatures.

Spruce, fir and pine trees fill taiga forests. Their waxy, needle-like leaves help the trees shake off heavy snowfalls.

Russian flying squirrels leap between trees in search of berries and leaves to eat.

Arctic foxes thrive in these cold forests. Their thick insulating fur protects against the cold.

Various peoples live in taiga forests. Many survive by hunting and fishing, or herding animals such as reindeer.

If trees are cut down, it takes a very long time for them to grow again.

FROM *the* TAIGA FOREST

Did you know that these products come from or are made from resources found in the taiga?

PAPER, CARDBOARD AND TISSUES: Most of our paper, card, toilet paper and tissue comes from the trees of the taiga.

OIL AND GAS: A lot of the world's oil and natural gas is found beneath the frozen ground of the taiga.

TIMBER: Softwood from the taiga is used to build windows, doors and floors.

The soil is poor quality and often frozen, meaning few plants grow.

Fire isn't always bad news for these forests. Tough bark protects older trees from damage by mild fires. For some trees, fire can even help them grow!

Great grey owls swoop down to prey on small rodents.

Bendy trunks help trees cope with high winds.

Grey wolves hunt here, preying on beavers, moose and other forest dwellers.

Moose roam the land. Their strong sense of smell helps them find food buried beneath the snow.

Arctic hares survive here with help from their fur. In the summer it is brown, and blends in with the trees, but when winter comes, it turns white, helping them hide in the snow.

In the summer, Bohemian waxwings perch on trees before snatching insects from mid-air.

Thousands of insects thrive in taiga wetlands. In the summer, billions of birds migrate here to breed and catch the creepy crawlies to feed their chicks.

Beavers swim and dive in the rivers to find tasty water plants to munch on.

Amur tigers, the world's largest cats, slink through these forest. Their stripy coats help to camouflage them amongst the trees.

TEMPERATE DECIDUOUS FORESTS

These forests are everchanging. They have four distinct seasons a year. In spring, leaves bud and flowers bloom. Summers are a bustle of activity, with birds singing and baby animals exploring. In autumn, the leaves of the trees turn fiery red and golden yellow, and animals rush about fattening themselves up for the cold to come. Finally, in winter, the trees lose their leaves, and animals migrate to warmer places or tuck themselves away in a long sleep called hibernation. All of this change means the animals and plants that live here are experts at adapting.

FROM *the* TEMPERATE FOREST

Did you know that these products come from or are made from resources found in temperate forests?

MAPLE SYRUP: The sap of maple trees is used to make sweet and delicious maple syrup.

NUTS: Hazelnuts, walnuts, chestnuts and pistachios all grow in temperate forests.

TRUFFLES: Dogs and pigs are used to sniff out valuable truffles (a rare type of mushroom) from beneath the leaf litter.

Insect-eating pileated woodpeckers hammer their beaks into the bark, in search of insects to snack on.

Below the canopy, small mammals such as squirrels scuttle through the leaves.

Many beetles, such as stag beetles, feed on the decaying wood and plants on the forest floor.

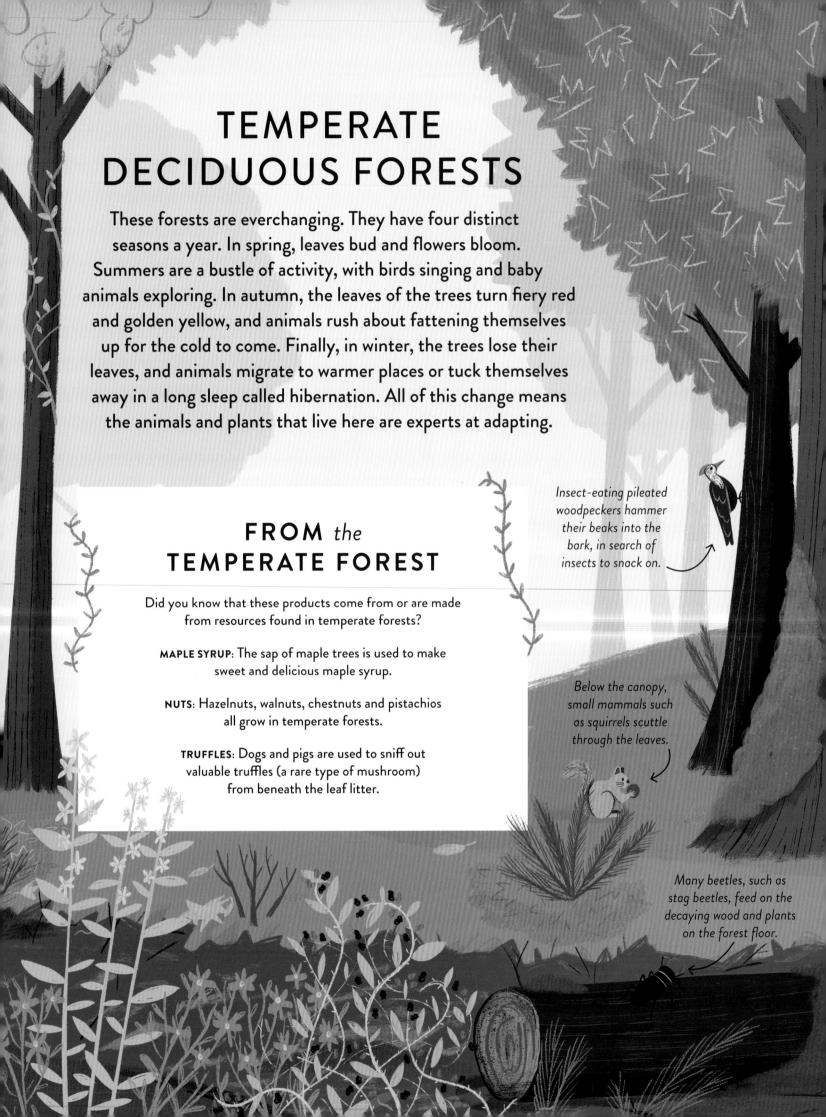

The most common trees are maples, oaks, beeches and chestnuts. The broad leaves of the trees allow sunlight to pass through the canopy, to the plants and shrubs on the forest floor.

Small hawks glide above the trees or perch under the canopy, on the lookout for prey below.

Trees are often covered in climbing vines such as ivy, which use their trunks to reach up towards the sunlight.

Black bears roam the forests, searching for fruit, nuts, honey and prey.

White-tailed deer munch on plants, nuts and twigs.

Bobcats hunt rodents, insects and deer. Their spotted grey-brown fur helps to camouflage them as they stalk their prey.

Racoons nest in the trees. Their five-fingered paws help them to climb up high.

Not many people live in temperate forests anymore. But they do visit them to enjoy the beauty and nature.

The leaf litter on the forest floor is broken down by fungi, bacteria, insects and worms, leaving a deep, fertile soil called humus.

Toads, frogs and newts hop and slink among the damp leaves.

13

THE PROBLEM *of* DEFORESTATION

As we have seen, the Earth is home to lots of different incredible forests. Sadly, all of these wonderful forests are affected by the same BIG problem: deforestation.

What is deforestation?

When trees are removed from the forest, so that the land can be used for other things, we call it 'deforestation'. It is not a new problem. Humans have been cutting down trees to make space for homes and farms for thousands of years. But the number of trees we are cutting down is growing all the time. In 2017, 40 football fields worth of tropical trees were lost EVERY MINUTE. If we don't make a change, forests could disappear from the Earth altogether. Let's take a look at how deforestation is affecting forests in different parts of the world.

Borneo

The forests on the island of Borneo, in Asia, are teeming with life. From orangutans and hornbills to plants that are made into life-saving drugs, many unique and important species call these forests home. In the 1970s, trees covered more than 75 percent of the island, but almost half of these have now been burned, replaced or chopped down. The main cause of deforestation in Borneo is the creation of palm oil plantations (see page 20).

1973

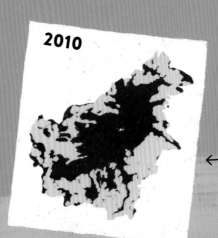

2010

These maps show how much forest was lost in Borneo between 1973 and 2010.

The Amazon

The Amazon is the world's largest tropical rainforest – it covers an area of South America that is more than twice the size of India! It is also home to 10 percent of all of the world's animals and plants. Forest here is mostly cleared for cattle ranching and soy plantations, but also to build towns, mines and dams. If deforestation rates don't slow down, over a quarter of the Amazon's trees will be gone by 2030.

1988

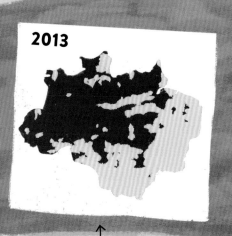
2013

These maps show how much forest was lost in the Amazon in the 25 years between 1988 and 2013.

FIRE, FIRE!

Deforestation doesn't always mean cutting down trees. Fires also cause deforestation. These can be started naturally by lightning strikes, or they can be started deliberately, to clear areas of forest, and then spread out of control. In 2019–2020, terrible forest fires in Australia destroyed millions of hectares of land and killed hundreds of millions of animals. It is normal for fires to break out in Australia every year, but scientists believe these fires were made worse by climate change (see page 28), which is creating hotter, drier weather.

(see page 28)

ELSEWHERE
in the WORLD

CANADA
Nearly a third of the world's taiga forest is found in Canada. Since 2000, almost 10 percent of this has been lost – an area bigger than the whole of Germany.

THE CONGO
The planet's second-largest tropical rainforest (after the Amazon) is the Congo Basin in Central Africa. Gorillas, chimpanzees and elephants all call this forest home. Deforestation is a big problem here, as trees are cleared to grow crops and dig mines.

THE UK
Most of the UK's temperate deciduous woodland was lost hundreds of years ago, before the Middle Ages. Once, the UK would have been almost entirely covered by trees, but today forest makes up just 13 percent of the land.

CHAPTER TWO
THE CAUSES OF DEFORESTATION

THERE ARE MANY REASONS PEOPLE CUT DOWN TREES.
Sometimes we want to use the trees themselves to make wood, paper or fuel; other times we want to use the forest land for something else instead, such as farming. Even if we live far away from forests, trees must be cut down to produce many of the things we use in our everyday lives. As the human population grows and its demands increase, more and more trees are lost.

PEOPLE, PEOPLE, EVERYWHERE

Think of all the people you know – your family, friends, teachers and so on. Can you count them all in your head? Now, imagine counting up the entire human population (all the people on Earth). How many humans do you think you would find? The answer is nearly 8 billion and this number is going up every day. That's a lot of people!

The people problem

Having more people in the world can be great: it can lead to more ideas and more great scientists, inventors and artists. But it can also pose problems. After all, the more people there are, the more resources and services those people need to survive. When a place becomes so full that it can't support the basic needs of all the people that live there, we call this overpopulation.

WHY *is the* POPULATION GROWING?

Thanks to amazing advances in medicine and more access to healthy foods, people are living longer and longer. A hundred years ago, most people lived until their 50s, but today we're living well into our 80s. The oldest a person has ever lived to so far is 122. That's a lot of birthday candles!

WHAT *can we* DO?

We can't simply stop building towns and cities for the people who need them – that wouldn't be fair. But there are ways to reduce the impact of overpopulation on forests.

Turn to pages 36–51 to find out how we can create protected areas where development is not allowed, and how we can manage forests in a way that does not cause them lasting harm.

How are forests affected?

When places become overpopulated, our world's forests are often the first victims. Trees are cut down and the wood is used to build new homes. The ground is dug up and paved over, and the precious space that was once bursting with plant and animal life is filled instead with people, houses and machines. The effects are huge: animals lose their homes, plants are destroyed, and the world becomes more polluted.

HOUSES
All people need a safe shelter to live in. When a population grows, more homes have to be built so more land has to be cleared.

OTHER BUILDINGS
People don't just need somewhere to live. They need hospitals, schools, shops, places to work and places to spend their time off. All of these take up more land.

WATER SUPPLY
Humans depend on water to survive, so it's really important that everyone has access to a clean water supply; this often means digging up the ground to lay new pipes.

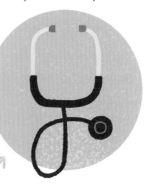

SEWERS
More people equals more poo and wee! If we didn't get rid of all this waste, people would get really sick – and let's face it, life would be pretty stinky. So, more sewers have to be built under the ground.

TRANSPORT
How do you get to the doctor's surgery, or the swimming pool? Most people use cars, bikes and public transport such as buses and trains. The more people there are, the more roads and train lines need to be paved and laid.

FARMLAND
People need food to eat. With all those new mouths to feed, more land must be set aside to grow crops and graze animals.

19

CROPS and CATTLE

It can be hard to understand how the food we eat can cause deforestation. After all, most of us aren't eating chunks of wood for dinner! But the truth is that anything that needs to be grown (such as crops) or reared (such as cows or chickens) needs space to be produced. And that's where forests come in.

So many mouths to feed

We all need food to survive. But in order to produce enough food for everyone, we need places to grow it. Unfortunately, a common solution is to cut down natural forests and replace them with pasture land (where animals are reared) and plantations (where only certain trees or plants are grown in order to produce foods such as coffee and sugar). Let's take a look at some specific examples of how human diets and habits are affecting forests.

PALM OIL

If you've cleaned your teeth and had breakfast today, then it's likely you've already used something that contains palm oil! From pizza to chocolate and soap to shampoo, palm oil-containing products are everywhere.

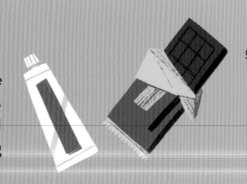

To meet this huge demand, more and more oil palm trees must be grown. To make space for them, other trees have to be cleared. In Sumatra in Indonesia, palm oil plantations now cover more than four times as much land as rainforests.

MEAT

Meat is a part of many peoples' diet, and as the world population increases, more and more animals are farmed to support the demand for more meat.

All these animals need land to live on and sadly, the world's forests are being cleared to create the space.

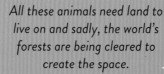

SOY

All the farm animals that are reared to produce meat for humans, need food to eat. One of the most common foods they are given is soy. We humans eat soy too but most soybeans (about 80 percent of them) are grown just to feed farm animals, including chickens, pigs and cows.

In order to produce enough soy, many forests and grasslands are cut down and ploughed over.

MONOCULTURE

Natural forests are brilliant patchworks of different trees, plants, rivers and streams. Their rich diversity allows them to support many different animals and people. Often in agriculture, forests are cut down and replaced with rows and rows of a single type of plant. This is called monoculture. Areas of monoculture support much less life than the forests they replace.

WHAT *can we* DO?

It's important to remember that not everyone has the opportunity to choose what they eat, and lots of people depend on farming for their livelihoods. Also, we definitely shouldn't all stop brushing our teeth! But there are lots of ways to reduce the impact of human diets and habits.

Turn to pages 36–51 to find out how we can farm more sustainably.

Turn to pages 52–57 to pick up tips on how you can make a difference, by eating less meat, buying sustainable palm oil, and more.

This means that many animals, such as orangutans, Sumatran tigers and Sumatran elephants are now running out of places to live.

Without the protection of the trees, the rich soil is soon washed away. After a while, grass stops growing.

The cattle then have to be moved to a new piece of land and yet more forest is cut down.

This means that local people who rely on the natural forests lose their livelihoods and homes, and native animals, including jaguars and giant anteaters, have nowhere to live.

TIMBER, PAPER, FUEL

Forests should be full of birdsong and buzzing insects. But in some forests, the loudest sounds are the roar of chainsaws and the crash of trees as they fall to the ground. These are the sounds of logging – cutting down trees in order to sell the wood. We use wood to make lots of our everyday products.

Why does the world like wood?

Wood is a fantastic material – it is natural, strong, hard, beautiful and easy to make into many different shapes. It is also biodegradable, meaning it breaks down in nature when you have finished using it.

Wood can be processed into building material such as planks (we call this timber) or it can be pulped and made into paper, cardboard, clothing and even food! It also makes a great fuel, either as firewood or charcoal. It's so great that for thousands of years – from Viking longships to the first planes – wood has helped humans advance and survive.

What's the problem?

The problem with the world's need for wood is that this material comes from trees – and that means trees have to be cut down. There are usually rules about how this can be done (see pages 48–49) but sadly they are not always followed. Forests are so huge that it is almost impossible to monitor all logging activity. Some loggers cut down trees in ways that break the rules, others enter forests illegally and cut down trees in protected areas.

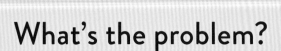

WHAT can we DO?

We obviously don't want to stop using wood altogether. But we need to make sure trees are harvested in the best way, and we can all help to support this.

Turn to pages 36–51 to find out how we can encourage good logging practices, tackle illegal logging and restore forests by replanting.

Turn to pages 52–57 to pick up tips on how you can make a difference – by using paper carefully, buying recycled or sustainably produced paper, planting new trees, and more.

How are trees cut down?

Trees can be cut down in different ways. Logging that is 'sustainable' is best, as it can carry on for a long time without causing great harm. Let's compare two different types of logging.

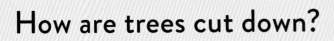

Animals are left homeless.

CLEAR-CUTTING

This means cutting all of the trees down in a certain area. This is a very damaging and unsustainable way of logging, as it completely destroys the forest ecosystem. If there are seeds in the ground the forest can eventually regrow after clear-cutting, but by then it will be too late for the animals that lived there.

Removing trees can result in soil erosion and cause silt to build up in local streams.

To get access to the forest, loggers need to clear roads and pathways through the trees.

SELECTIVE LOGGING

This is where only the biggest trees, which are the most useful to humans, are felled. By only cutting down old trees, and leaving the young ones, this type of logging allows the forest to regrow. If it is done properly, it can be a sustainable way of logging.

Only cutting down big trees gives younger trees more space and sunlight to grow and leaves enough food and shelter for animals.

Selective logging still changes the delicate balance of the forest. The huge trees can also uproot others when they fall. But if it is done carefully, this type of logging does not cause long-term damage to the forest.

BURIED TREASURE

Did you know that the ground beneath our feet can be extremely precious? That's right, lurking deep beneath the mud, sand and soil are hidden treasures such as oil, coal and gas (known as fossil fuels), minerals and metals. These buried resources have become crucial to our modern-day lives and they are mined all over the world.

Why is mining so damaging to forests?

Mining can be very damaging for the trees, animals and people that live nearby. Let's take a look at some of the effects that mining has on our forests.

GETTING TO THE MINE

If the mine is deep in the forest, trees must be cut down to create roads. These roads are sometimes used by illegal loggers and poachers (people who hunt or trap wild animals), giving them easier access into parts of the forest that were previously very hard to get to. If the mines are really big, trees may also be cut down to build housing and airports for the people who work at the mines.

DIGGING THE HOLE

Valuable resources are often found deep underground. Enormous holes have to be dug to get to them. To make it easier to dig, all of the trees on the surface above the mine are cut down. Some mines even use explosives to help them dig large craters.

WHAT *are we* MINING?

Many different resources are found deep in the earth beneath forests. Cobalt (a blue-coloured metal) is used to make batteries found in phones and other devices. It is mostly mined in Africa, and is so valuable that people often call it 'blue gold'.

Another valuable resource is oil, which we use to heat our homes and power our vehicles. Oil is found in many places in the world, including tropical rainforests.

WHAT *can we* DO?

We all use mined resources every day – to power our cars, heat our homes and operate our electronic devices. So how can we help to protect forests from the effects of mining?

Turn to pages 36–51 to find out how we can tackle some of the problems.

Turn to pages 52–57 to pick up tips on how you can make a difference, by looking after your electronic devices, using less fossil fuels, and more.

LEAKS AND POLLUTION
Often the resources that are dug up from the ground are poisonous to the environment. Sometimes mining waste washes into forest rivers, or is dumped illegally, which is very dangerous to the animals and people who depend on those waterways for fresh water.

THE WILDLIFE
Mining can have a huge impact on surrounding wildlife. In the Democratic Republic of Congo in Africa, for example, there are many mineral mines. These mines are in an area that is home to the eastern lowland gorilla. Today, much of the forest these gorillas once lived in has been cut down to make way for mines, and the gorillas are critically endangered.

REGROWING THE FOREST
Even after mining is finished, it can take a very long time for the forest to recover. The waterways are often badly polluted, and the ground is scarred by the mining activity, making it difficult for the forest to return.

CHAPTER THREE
THE EFFECTS OF DEFORESTATION

TREES ARE VITALLY IMPORTANT.
They provide a home and food for the billions of animals and people that live in the forest, and they are the planet's lungs, using up carbon dioxide and releasing oxygen. When we cut down trees, we affect the delicate balance of our planet. Cutting down trees is just as bad for Earth as driving cars and flying planes. If we cut down too many, the world will be changed forever.

CLIMATE CHANGE

Forests are deeply connected to our planet's climate.
They help to stop the Earth from getting too hot or too cold,
and they affect cloud formation, winds and the water cycle.
They also help prevent dangerous gases from building up in the
atmosphere. Deforestation means that there are fewer trees to
do all this vital work, and this is affecting our planet's climate.

What is climate change?

Climate change is the process of our world's weather
and temperature patterns changing over time. In the last
century, Earth has warmed up very quickly, by around 1 degree
Celsius (we call this 'global warming'). This may not sound like much,
but just 1 degree has already had HUGE effects on our planet:

- Ice sheets and glaciers are shrinking.
- Sea levels are rising.
- Floods and droughts are becoming more common.
- Extreme weather such as hurricanes
  and tornadoes are happening more often.
- Wildfires are bigger and more ferocious.

What's causing the heat?

It is normal for Earth's temperatures to change over time, but these changes usually take place over thousands
or millions of years. The recent quick rise in the Earth's temperature is because of human actions. Why is this?

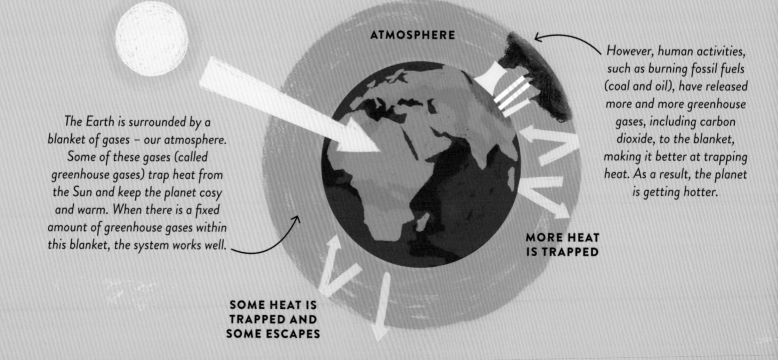

ATMOSPHERE

The Earth is surrounded by a
blanket of gases – our atmosphere.
Some of these gases (called
greenhouse gases) trap heat from
the Sun and keep the planet cosy
and warm. When there is a fixed
amount of greenhouse gases within
this blanket, the system works well.

However, human activities,
such as burning fossil fuels
(coal and oil), have released
more and more greenhouse
gases, including carbon
dioxide, to the blanket,
making it better at trapping
heat. As a result, the planet
is getting hotter.

MORE HEAT
IS TRAPPED

SOME HEAT IS
TRAPPED AND
SOME ESCAPES

Where do trees come in?

Almost all plants use carbon dioxide (one of the greenhouse gases) as they grow. This removes carbon dioxide from the atmosphere, which helps to prevent the planet from warming up. Trees are particularly good at this – a forest will store 100 times more carbon than a field of crops of the same size. One of the best ways we can fight climate change is to plant more trees!

When we chop trees down, they can no longer remove carbon dioxide from the air, but that's not all. They also release all the carbon dioxide they had already stored. Deforestation releases more than 1.4 billion tonnes of carbon dioxide every year.

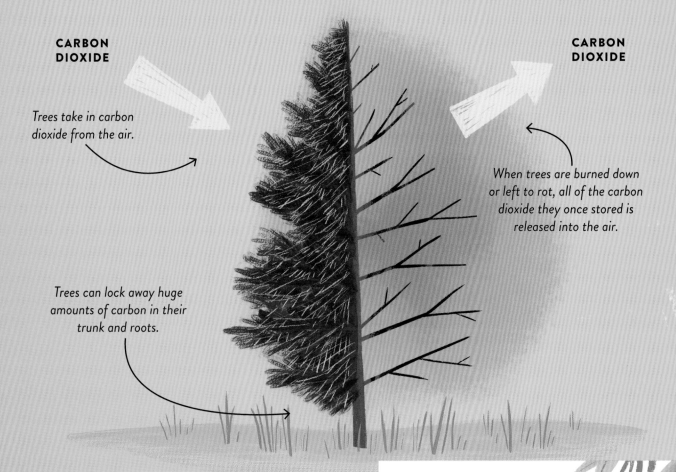

CARBON DIOXIDE

Trees take in carbon dioxide from the air.

Trees can lock away huge amounts of carbon in their trunk and roots.

CARBON DIOXIDE

When trees are burned down or left to rot, all of the carbon dioxide they once stored is released into the air.

WEATHER *or* CLIMATE?

The difference between weather and climate is all about time. Weather changes daily, whereas climate is the average weather in a place over a number of years.

WHAT *can we* DO?

Protecting our forests is an important part of fighting climate change. There are lots of things – big and small – we can all do to help protect the future of our planet.

Turn to pages 36–51 to find out what people, organisations and scientists are doing to help fight climate change.

Turn to pages 52–57 to pick up tips on how you can make a difference – by buying less stuff, walking and cycling more, making your voice heard, and more!

NATURE OFF-BALANCE

Did you know that lots of the things we take for granted, such as rain, clean air and healthy soil, only exist because of trees? Trees keep the planet working as it should – without them, the world would be a very different place.

What happens in a healthy forest?

In a healthy forest, each part of every tree plays an important role in keeping the environment in balance.

Water is released from the leaves into the air. This will eventually form clouds and fall as rain, giving plants and animals water to drink.

Leaves release oxygen, which animals need to breathe, and filter harmful pollution.

Leaves intercept rainwater, preventing too much of it from falling to the ground at once and causing flooding.

The leafy canopy shades the ground beneath, keeping it cool and preventing moisture evaporating from the soil.

Hundreds of animals, big and small, make their homes in trees. In the delicate balance of nature, every one of these creatures is important. They spread seeds, pollinate plants and fertilise the soil with their droppings.

The trees take water from the ground and use it to grow.

Roots anchor the soil, preventing it from being washed away into rivers and streams.

When leaves fall, they rot and provide the soil with lots of nutrients that help plants to grow.

What happens if there are no trees?

When trees are cut down, the balance is lost. Very quickly, land that was once lush and green can turn into empty desert.

DROUGHTS
Without leaves to release water into the air, less rain falls. This can result in shortages of water, called droughts.

POOR SOIL
With no rotting leaves to fertilise the soil, and no shady canopy to prevent moisture from evaporating, the Sun dries out the earth. Nothing new can grow in this barren, dusty soil.

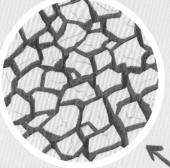

FLOODS
Without trees to help slow down rainwater, water can flow quicker into rivers and streams. When the shallow rivers receive more rainwater, they are more likely to flood.

LANDSLIDES
Without tree roots to hold the soil in place, landslides can become more common. These are very dangerous to people, animals and plants.

SILTY RIVERS
The dusty soil is easily blown away by wind or washed away into rivers and streams. Rivers become silty and shallow, which makes it hard for some fish and other river animals to survive. The rivers can also be poisonous for people and animals relying on the water.

ANIMALS IN DANGER
When trees disappear, the animals that lived in them disappear too. The plants that relied on these creatures for pollinating them or spreading their seeds cannot survive once they are gone.

PEOPLE at RISK

For thousands of years, people have lived in forests without damaging them. These are often indigenous communities – the first people who ever lived there. These people have a deep connection with the forest. They rely on it to provide them with a home and food, but they also know that if they take too much from the forest, there will be nothing left for their children.

What are the threats?

Not all people are so respectful of the forest. Companies and governments sometimes take the resources they want in a way that threatens to destroy the forest completely. When they do this, they also threaten the culture and way of life of the indigenous people who call it home. Let's take a look at how indigenous people are affected in two different forests.

In the tropical forest

Around a million indigenous people live in the Amazon rainforest. These people are split into many small groups. Some of these groups have never had contact with the world outside their forest! The Awá people live deep in the Brazilian Amazon. Every day, illegal loggers move deeper into Awá lands. Awá people have been shot and killed by loggers while trying to protect their forest. If the Awá people run out of forest, they will lose the only way of life they have ever known.

The Awá's shelters, hammocks, clothing and tools are all made from forest materials.

The Awá are completely dependent on the forest, hunting and gathering everything they need to survive.

Awá people often keep orphaned baby forest animals as pets.

In the taiga

Northern Scandinavia and Russia are home to a group of an indigenous people called the Saami, who have used taiga forests for many centuries. Once, many Saami roamed the taiga with their reindeer herds, but now only around 1 in 10 Saami live in this way. The area of taiga forest available for them to graze their reindeer is getting smaller all the time. It is threatened by logging, mining and the building of new roads and train lines. If the Saami can no longer herd their reindeer, they will lose much of their culture and traditions too.

The Saami people have a great respect for and understanding of the natural world.

The Saami use the forest for breeding and rearing reindeer, as well as hunting and gathering firewood.

Some Saami people are nomadic, which means they move from place to place with their reindeer herd. They stay in tents called 'laavu'.

WE ALL NEED TREES!

It is not only the people who live within forests that suffer the effects of deforestation. The water we drink, the air we breathe and the animals and plants we eat are all affected by deforestation in some way. If the world loses its trees, people everywhere will suffer.

ANIMALS in DANGER

When forests are cut down, animals that depend on them for food and shelter can struggle to survive. In the last 40 years, the number of animals living in the world's forests has more than halved. Some types of animal have lost so much of their forest home that they are now endangered, which means that they are at risk of becoming extinct (disappearing completely from the Earth). Imagine a world without gorillas, jaguars or koalas – if we don't stop cutting down trees, these animals could be lost forever. Let's meet a few of the animals whose future is threatened by deforestation.

In the tropical forest

There are few animals better suited for life in a tropical rainforest than the orangutan. Swinging gracefully through the branches by day and building treetop nests to sleep in at night, this creature spends almost its entire life in the trees. But the rainforests that orangutans live in, on the islands of Borneo and Sumatra in Southeast Asia, are some of the fastest disappearing forests in the world. New roads through the forest also allow poachers to enter and steal baby orangutans to be sold as pets. Unless we do something about these threats, orangutans are likely to disappear from the wild within 30 years.

PLANTS in TROUBLE

It's not just animal species that are under threat. Around two-thirds of the world's plant species are found in tropical rainforests. When forests are cut down, some plant species are lost forever, including some that we may never even have known existed!

WHAT can we DO?

We all want to protect the incredible animals and plants that live in Earth's forests. But how?

Turn to pages 36–51 to find out how conservation, ecotourism, forest rangers and technology can all help protect forest species.

Turn to pages 52–57 to pick up tips on how your everyday actions can help to look after forests and the animals that live in them.

In the temperate forest

As night falls, northern spotted owls swoop silently below the treeline, hunting for prey. These threatened owls live in the oak-pine forests of western North America, which have lots of different plants and large, older trees to roost in. But in many places, these healthy ancient forests are being cut down for timber and replanted with younger trees. Northern spotted owls can't survive in younger forests, so their numbers are falling. It can take up to 100 years for the forest to recover enough to support all of the wildlife that once lived there.

In the taiga

Prowling through the forests of north-eastern Russia and China, the Amur tiger travels huge distances in search of prey. Its huge paws stop it from sinking into the deep snow and its thick fur protects it against the freezing cold. Over 95 percent of the forest that these tigers once lived in has been destroyed by humans. When the tigers stray onto land where people now live, they are often killed. It is thought there may be less than 600 of these tigers left in the wild.

Already lost...

Sadly it is already too late for these animals – they have all become extinct because of deforestation.

CUBAN IVORY-BILLED WOODPECKER

Last seen in the 1980s, this woodpecker died out when Cuba's old forests were cleared and converted to sugar plantations.

SPIX'S MACAW

This beautiful parrot has been extinct in the wild since around 2000, due to the destruction of its Brazilian forest home.

MADEIRAN LARGE WHITE BUTTERFLY

The loss of laurel forests on Madeira, a Portuguese island, meant this butterfly had nowhere left to live. It has not been seen since the 1980s.

CHAPTER FOUR
THE SOLUTIONS TO DEFORESTATION

**'THE BEST TIME TO PLANT A TREE
WAS 20 YEARS AGO.
THE SECOND-BEST TIME IS NOW.'**
Chinese proverb.

Fortunately, it's not too late to reverse the effects of deforestation. But we need to act NOW! For our forests to survive and thrive, we need to find clever solutions, use the latest technology and involve lots of different people. Luckily, there are thousands of people all over the world who have dedicated their lives to saving forests. From farmers and journalists to conservationists and scientists, everyone has a role to play in protecting our trees.

PRESERVING *the* WILD

Scientists think that there are around 3 trillion trees on Earth today – that's a huge number, but before humans started to cut them down there were TWICE as many as that! It's very important to protect the trees that are left. Thankfully, there are lots of practical solutions being used all over the world to preserve our planet's forests. Let's take a look...

Conservation

Preserving our plants, animals and natural areas is called conservation. There are many different kinds of conservationists, including scientists, who work to protect our forests and the animals and plants that live there. They use methods such as breeding programmes (where endangered animals are bred in wildlife reserves) and they do research, which they share with the world (see page 46).

In the 1970s the Rodrigues fruit bat species was on the brink of extinction because the forests they lived in were cut down. Thanks to conservation efforts, there are now more than 20,000 of these little bats today.

Restoring forests

If they are left completely alone, forests can eventually restore themselves. But it's possible to speed up that process and give them a helping hand. Tree-planting projects are a great example. These projects are organised all over the world and allow people, young and old, to get involved. Trees can be planted in areas that have lost their trees (we call this reforestation) or in places that have not had trees for a long time (we call this afforestation).

The charity Trees for Cities has planted over a million trees in towns and cities in the UK and other countries. Thousands of volunteers help to plant trees in local parks, schools, community orchards and other urban spaces.

Ecotourism

Did you know that tourists can help save forests? Ecotourism (where people travel to natural areas with a goal to help preserve them) provides jobs and money for local people and governments. This makes the forests that the tourists want to visit valuable, and keeps them safe.

Protected areas

Governments help preserve forests by creating protected areas, where activities such as logging, mining and hunting wildlife are totally forbidden. This keeps the people, animals and plants of the forest safe from harm. There are around 200,000 protected areas around the world today.

National parks and reserves, such as Redwood National Park in the US, are a type of protected area.

The Achuar people are an indigenous rainforest community. They have depended on the forest for their survival for hundreds of years and know how to live in the forest without causing harm to it.

Community forests

Sometimes governments give protected land over to local communities or indigenous people to run for themselves. The community are then responsible for the decision-making and planning of the forests and are free to manage them as they see fit. Because they live locally, they treat the forest respectfully and do not take too many of its resources.

TACKLING LOGGING
and MINING

The world is not going to stop using products that are made from wood or dug up from mines, so we must make sure we get these products in a way that causes the least possible harm to forests. The best way to do this is to support products that are made in sustainable ways, and to stop people logging and mining illegally.

Encourage sustainable logging

As we've seen, some methods of logging are more sustainable than others (see page 23). By choosing to buy wood and paper products that we know have been cut down in a sustainable way, we can all help to support good logging practices. Logos and labels make it clear which products are good to buy.

The Forest Stewardship Council (FSC)® is an international organisation that checks that forests have been managed in a way that treats people and the environment in a responsible way. Products that have passed their tests display the FSC tick tree logo. This book is made on FSC paper – see if you can find the logo!

Support local people

The people who cut down trees in unsustainable ways often do this to earn a living for themselves and their families. They might be working for a big company, and just following orders. Or they might be logging or mining illegally, usually because they desperately need the money to pay for food or health care. We need to make sure that local people who depend on these activities for their income don't suffer. One way to do this is by offering training or providing them with different jobs.

The Chainsaw Buyback program, set up in Indonesia in 2017, allows people who make their money from illegal logging to swap their chainsaws for loans and training that will allow them to start new lives as farmers.

Use technology

It can be difficult to know when illegal logging and mining are happening, because forests are so huge. But there are some clever ways we can use technology to help us.

Flying drones over the forest allows the authorities to look in hard-to-reach areas and spot illegal logging or mining activity.

In 2013, inventor and explorer Topher White created a system that could listen out for the sounds of illegal logging and send a message to alert the authorities. His invention used solar cells and old mobile phones, which were programmed to recognise the sound of chainsaws up to 1.6 km away. It was so successful in Indonesia that it is now also used across Africa and South America.

Track forest products

If we can't track where our products come from, it is difficult to know if they were made sustainably or not. The people managing forests don't always keep careful records. But technology is making it easier. Engineers have started creating apps that can store information about individual trees, allowing us to track where each one starts and ends up.

One day, as technology develops, people buying a wooden product may be able to know exactly which forest it came from at the click of a button.

Employ forest rangers

Rangers patrol forests to protect all of the animals and plants living in them. They are very brave, working day and night to prevent trees and animals being illegally taken away.

TACKLING FARMING

In the next 30 years, the number of people in the world is likely to grow by around TWO BILLION. That's a lot more people to feed. We can't keep cutting down trees to make more land for growing crops or grazing animals. Instead, we need to start farming in a way that protects our planet, and its forests, for future generations. We call this sustainable farming. Let's take a look at some of the ways we can farm more sustainably.

Agroforestry

When we think of farmland, we normally think of big fields covered in just one kind of crop. But farmland doesn't have to be like this. In a type of farming called 'agroforestry', trees are planted between rows of crops or in fields where animals graze. The trees help to make the soil more fertile, meaning crops grow better, and they also give forest animals somewhere to live.

Zero Deforestation Commitments

One solution to deforestation is to get companies to be more responsible and stop buying and selling products that are farmed on deforested land. A Zero Deforestation Commitment (ZDC) is a promise made by a company that no forests have been destroyed to make their products. This can either mean that no trees have been cut down at all, or that trees have been cut down but then replaced with new ones.

One of the first ZDCs, called the 'Amazon Soy Moratorium', was signed in 2006 by almost all of the soy traders (people who buy and sell soy) in the Amazon. They promised not to buy soybeans grown on land that had been recently deforested, and they stuck to their promise! As a result, the amount of soy that was grown on deforested land dropped from 30 percent to just 1 percent in less than 10 years.

Protein alternatives

Protein-rich foods, which include meat, are an important part of our diet. But rearing big animals like cows takes a lot of land, water and food (often soya). One solution is for all of us to eat less meat and replace it with protein that comes from different foods, such as grains, lentils, beans and nuts.

For thousands of years, people all over the world have added protein to their diets by eating insects. From gooey ants that taste like honey to chewy, creamy beetle larvae, insects can be farmed quickly, in a way that causes very little damage to the environment. In Cambodia, deep-fried tarantulas can be bought on the side of the road as a quick snack.

Sustainable palm oil

Huge areas of Asian rainforest have been cleared to grow palm oil (see pages 20–21) and millions of farmers depend on it for a living. The world is not going to stop using palm oil any time soon, so it is important it is grown responsibly. Here are two ways the world can help:

1. Encourage producers to grow their oil palm trees in a way that is sustainable. This means only using land that has already been cleared. It also means protecting endangered animals and working with local communities.

In some sustainable palm oil plantations in Indonesia, forest is set aside for wildlife. This helps to protect endangered animals such as pangolins.

2. Encourage individuals and businesses to only buy sustainable palm oil.

Conservationists working at the UK's Chester Zoo ran a successful campaign to make Chester the world's first 'Sustainable Palm Oil City'. They convinced more than fifty organisations in the city to commit to using sustainable palm oil – and now their goal is to make sure that everyone else in the city makes the same pledge too. To help people, they have produced a handy shopping list of products that use sustainable palm oil.

GETTING TECHNICAL

Our modern world is full of technology. In some ways, making and powering all this technology is to blame for some of the big problems facing our planet, such as climate change. But technology can also be used for good in the fight to save our forests. Here are some of the creative ideas that scientists, designers and engineers have come up with.

Renewable energy

Some of the world's energy comes from the oil and gas found beneath forests, or from wood and charcoal that is burnt for cooking and heating. But scientists have developed other ways we can make energy that do not involve destroying our forests. Solar panels use the power of the Sun to produce energy. The power of the wind and water can be used, too. The great thing about these types of energy is that they are renewable, meaning they never get used up!

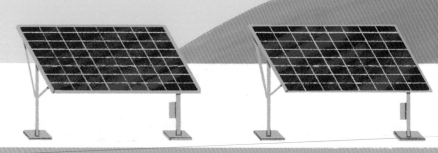

Artificial photosynthesis

Plants are energy-making machines. Through photosynthesis, they turn carbon dioxide, water and sunlight into energy. Scientists have now worked out how to do this too! It is difficult and expensive at the moment, but one day it may become a useful source of energy – and it doesn't involve destroying any forests.

Satellites

We need to know where deforestation is happening in order to try to stop it. At one time, getting this information was very hard. But now we can see forests from space, using machines called satellites, which orbit the Earth and take pictures as they fly overhead. This shows us exactly where forest is being lost, how much and how quickly.

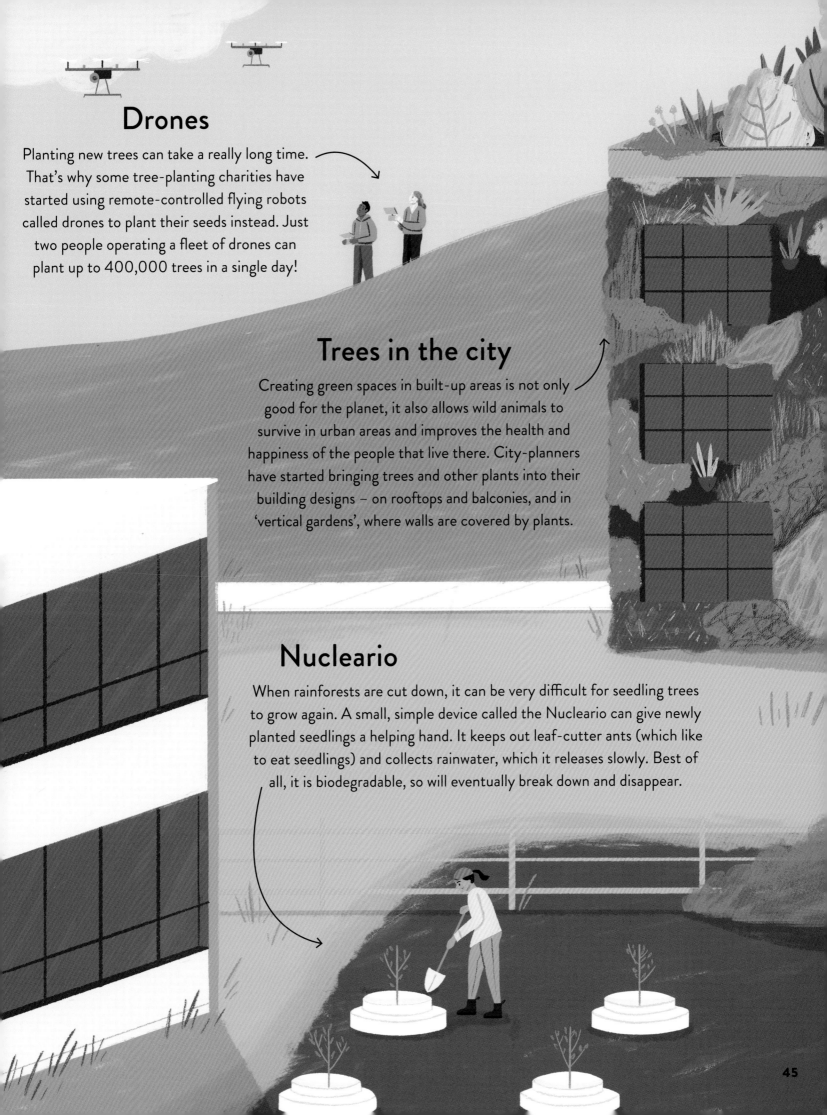

Drones

Planting new trees can take a really long time. That's why some tree-planting charities have started using remote-controlled flying robots called drones to plant their seeds instead. Just two people operating a fleet of drones can plant up to 400,000 trees in a single day!

Trees in the city

Creating green spaces in built-up areas is not only good for the planet, it also allows wild animals to survive in urban areas and improves the health and happiness of the people that live there. City-planners have started bringing trees and other plants into their building designs – on rooftops and balconies, and in 'vertical gardens', where walls are covered by plants.

Nucleario

When rainforests are cut down, it can be very difficult for seedling trees to grow again. A small, simple device called the Nucleario can give newly planted seedlings a helping hand. It keeps out leaf-cutter ants (which like to eat seedlings) and collects rainwater, which it releases slowly. Best of all, it is biodegradable, so will eventually break down and disappear.

SHARING *the* FACTS

When you have all the facts, it's easy to see why cutting down trees is a big mistake. But unless people understand exactly why forests are so important and just how damaging it can be to cut them down, deforestation is never going to stop. Let's find out how sharing the facts is helping us to save forests.

Science

One way knowledge is being shared is through science! Large areas of the world's forests have never been explored. Who knows what secrets are lurking within them, waiting to be discovered? Scientists exploring these forests find out about the incredible animals and plants that live there and then share their findings with the world. Their research helps us learn about amazing plants that can be used to treat diseases such as cancer, and tells us which animals and plants are in danger and need protecting.

In the Brazilian Atlantic Forest, scientists are studying many rare species, such as the maned sloth, in the hope that they can learn better how to protect them.

News, TV and books

The media is another way that the facts about deforestation are being shared. News articles give us up-to-date statistics about how much forest has been lost. Documentaries and books (like this one!) can explain in even more detail why deforestation is happening. They allow people from all over the world to understand the problem and see how their own actions affect trees thousands of miles away. This can lead to people changing their behaviour, from the products they buy to the food that they eat.

Learning from each other

The people who know forests best are the people who live or work in them and care about protecting them – scientists, experts and indigenous people. By sharing what they know, they can help to keep forests safe.

Sometimes, people who live near forests and earn money from selling forest products may not realise why deforestation is so bad for their communities and for the planet. By sharing the facts with them, scientists and experts can help them understand the value of their forests. For example, the forest might help to keep the local river clean, or it may be home to animals not found anywhere else. Local people can also learn about other ways they can make a living from the forest without harming it, such as from ecotourism (see page 39).

The world can also learn from the indigenous people who live in forests. These communities often have thousands of years' worth of knowledge and experience of managing forests sustainably.

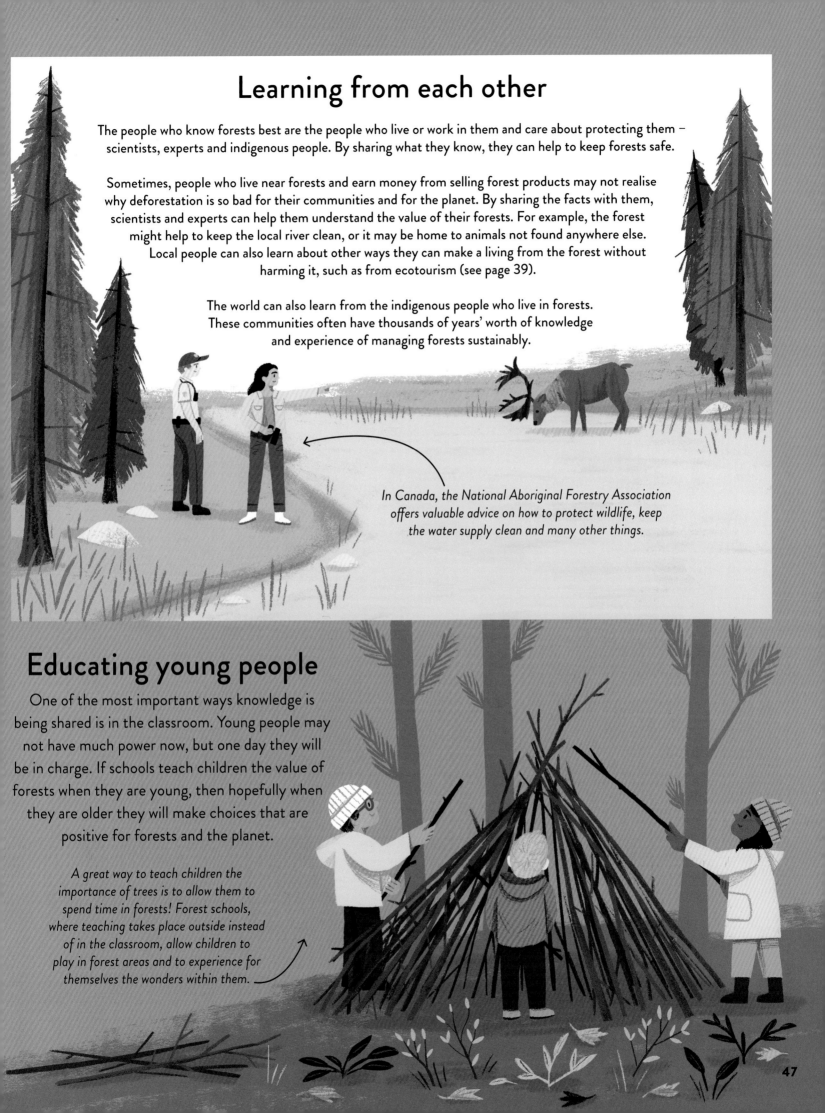

In Canada, the National Aboriginal Forestry Association offers valuable advice on how to protect wildlife, keep the water supply clean and many other things.

Educating young people

One of the most important ways knowledge is being shared is in the classroom. Young people may not have much power now, but one day they will be in charge. If schools teach children the value of forests when they are young, then hopefully when they are older they will make choices that are positive for forests and the planet.

A great way to teach children the importance of trees is to allow them to spend time in forests! Forest schools, where teaching takes place outside instead of in the classroom, allow children to play in forest areas and to experience for themselves the wonders within them.

47

LAWS and RULES

One of the best ways to tackle deforestation is through laws and rules that protect forests – without them, anybody could cut down as many trees as they liked, and we might have no forests left at all! Laws and agreements make sure individuals, companies and countries all follow the rules and are responsible for their actions.

Let's take a look at some examples of different laws, rules and agreements that are helping fight deforestation today.

Government permits

In every country, the government can set aside areas of forest to be protected (see page 39). In these areas, cutting down trees is forbidden by law. But governments can also decide which areas of forest can be chopped down and used for logging, mining or farming. Any company that wants to cut down forest must apply to the government for a permit, which gives them permission and sets out the rules. For example, a logging permit will say:

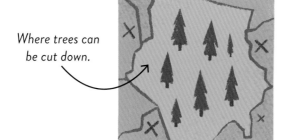

Where trees can be cut down.

x 100

How many trees can be cut down. (This is called a 'quota'.)

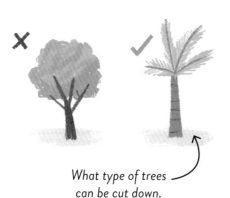

✗ ✓

What type of trees can be cut down.

The way the trees should be cut down.

Keeping indigenous communities safe

Sometimes, it is not governments or big organisations that lead to laws being made that protect forests – it is the actions of individuals or small groups of people. The Waorani people are an indigenous community from the forests of Ecuador. When the government tried to sell their land to oil companies, the Waorani people decided to take them to court. In 2019, they won their case, and the court ruled it was against the law to sell the Waorani's land without asking them. This means the Waorani's forest, and their way of life, is now protected by law.

Helping prevent climate change

In 2016, virtually all the countries in the world signed an agreement called the Paris Climate Accord, in which they promised to take steps to prevent climate change. These steps included reducing greenhouse gases and taking action to stop Earth's temperatures from rising out of control. This agreement makes governments responsible for looking after their forests and controlling rates of deforestation.

Protecting plants and animals

Some laws and agreements protect the plants and animals that live in forests. CITES (which is short for 'The Convention on International Trade in Endangered Species of Wild Fauna and Flora') is an agreement between more than 180 countries, which started in 1975. Its aim is to control the trade of endangered plants and animals so that this does not threaten their survival. Under the agreement, it is illegal to trade the wood from hundreds of types of tree unless you have special permits. This means fewer people will cut down these trees as they will not be able to sell them.

MAHOGANY

POISON DART FROG

PEOPLE POWER

No matter how bad things get for forests, they cannot speak up for themselves and ask for protection. So, it is down to conservationists, charities and brave individuals to lend their voices to the trees. Let's meet some of the incredible people and groups who have made a stand.

Patricia Wright

In 1986, American lemur expert Patricia Wright travelled to Madagascar to search for the greater bamboo lemur, which many people thought was extinct. Not only did she discover the species she was searching for, she also found a new species entirely! Patricia soon realised that the forest her lemurs lived in was under threat from logging. With her help, Ranomafana National Park was created, which protects trees as well as 12 different species of lemur.

Wangari Muta Maathai

In 1977, Kenyan activist Wangari Muta Maathai set up a campaign called the Green Belt Movement. This campaign encouraged African women to plant trees around their local farms, schools and churches and to care about environmental issues. Wangari's movement led to the planting of over 50 million trees in Kenya and made her the first African woman to win the Nobel Peace Prize, in 2004.

25 voices against deforestation

In 2018, 25 young people (aged between 7 and 26) from Colombia, who called themselves '25 voices against deforestation', sued their government for failing to protect the Amazon rainforest from deforestation. The group argued that indigenous people, future generations and nature itself all had a right to a healthy climate. They won their case and the Colombian government was ordered to create an action plan to protect the rainforest.

The Temiar people

When a logging company began cutting down the forest where the Temiar people lived, they decided to do something about it. The Temiar people have lived in the rainforests of Malaysia for generations, and do not want their homes, hunting grounds and way of life to be destroyed. When the government ignored their plea for help, they decided to build roadblocks to stop the logging trucks from entering the forest. The logging company went to court demanding the barricades be removed. But the Temiar people won the legal battle, and continue to fight for the protection of their land.

Greta Thunberg

In August 2018, Swedish teenager Greta Thunberg decided to miss school in order to hold a strike outside parliament. She was protesting about climate change – one of the biggest consequences of deforestation. Since then she has inspired young people all around the world to take action for the planet, proving that one person's voice can have a global impact.

Felix Finkbeiner

Plant for the Planet is an international charity created in 2007 after a German schoolboy, Felix Finkbeiner, came up with the idea that the world's children could plant one million trees. In three years, the charity achieved their goal, so Felix set a new one – to plant a TRILLION new trees! Today, the charity is working to achieve this goal and has over 70,000 child ambassadors who help encourage others to take action and protect the planet.

CHAPTER FIVE
WHAT YOU CAN DO

YOU CAN HELP, TOO!

When you're just one person, standing
up to governments and big companies,
or changing world habits can seem like
an impossible task. But even if you're not a
scientist or an inventor, you are never too small
to make a difference. Every action you take has an
effect on the people, plants and animals around you.
It's up to you to decide what kind of effect that will
be. If enough of us work together to make the same
positive actions, we can achieve huge things!

CHANGE *your* HABITS

We don't always think about how our everyday actions affect forests thousands of miles away. But every time we switch on a light or throw a piece of paper in the rubbish bin, we could be using up valuable forest resources. So, how can YOU change your habits to help forests? By making these small changes, you can make a big difference.

Forget fossil fuels

We have learned how mining for fossil fuels such as oil, coal and gas can be bad for forests, but how can we use less of them?

- Try to walk or cycle on short journeys, instead of going by car. Many cars are powered by fossil fuels.

- Use and buy less plastic. Plastic is made from oil.

- In your family, think about fun holidays you can have that don't involve flying. Travelling by plane uses up lots of fossil fuels.

- Ask your grown-up to find out about companies that supply renewable energy.

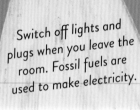

Switch off lights and plugs when you leave the room. Fossil fuels are used to make electricity.

Encourage everyone in your house to put on an extra jumper instead of turning up the heating. Many central heating systems use gas to power them.

Plant trees

Changing your behaviour doesn't just mean stopping habits that harm forests – it can also mean starting new helpful habits or hobbies. Why not join a local tree planting group, or plant some trees in your garden or at school? They may start as tiny saplings, but one day those trees will be taller than you are; they will provide a home for lots of different animals, as well as capture carbon dioxide and provide clean air for us to breathe.

Buy less!

We live in a throwaway world. We are used to constantly buying new things and getting rid of old ones when they are broken or when we get bored of them. But it wasn't always this way. Not that long ago, people made things by hand and fixed them when they were broken. They were happy to have fewer things and looked after them carefully. You can do this too! Taking good care of your things means you will need to buy fewer new ones.

- Use things until they are completely worn out.

- Take care of your electronic devices. If they break, get them fixed instead of throwing them away.

- Before buying something new, think about whether you really need it. If you do, turn to pages 56–57 for tips on how to buy responsibly.

See if you can use the same pencil until it becomes a tiny little stub!

Learn how to mend things, such as torn clothes and holey socks!

Waste less!

Instead of throwing things away when you are finished, could you think of a creative way to use them again?

- Use old toilet rolls and cardboard packaging for craft projects.

- Use paper on both sides. You can even use the same piece of paper multiple times, until all the white spaces are filled.

- Think about donating your family's old mobile phones to a conservation project, such as Topher White's (page 41).

- If you can't reuse something or give it away, find out if you can recycle it before putting it in the bin. It takes much less energy to make new products from recycled waste than from raw materials.

Use your paintings and drawings as wrapping paper for presents.

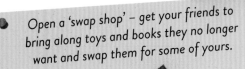

Open a 'swap shop' – get your friends to bring along toys and books they no longer want and swap them for some of yours.

BUY RESPONSIBLY

Consumers (people who buy things) have a lot of power. By looking carefully at labels, and thinking about where the things we buy come from, we can choose to buy things that are produced in ways that are kind to the planet and forests, and avoid things that are produced in ways that cause harm.

Buy sustainable products

If you need to buy products that come from forests, then it is important to make sure that they are produced in a sustainable way. You can check the packaging for this information, or look online. By choosing only to buy sustainably produced products, it sends a message to loggers and farmers that we care about trees and the planet. If enough people refuse to buy products that are made in unsustainable ways, eventually loggers and farmers will realise they need to change their methods.

PALM OIL
Look out for companies and products that only use sustainable palm oil. Palm oil can be very well hidden in labels; 'vegetable oil' or 'vegetable fat', for example, are both different ways of saying 'palm oil'. Where you can, try to choose products that list 'sustainable palm oil' or, better still, 'no palm oil' instead.

PAPER AND WOOD
If you are buying wood or paper products, look out for the FSC logo. This will tell you that they were produced using forest materials from responsible sources.

Buy meat responsibly

Forests are sometimes cut down to graze cattle or to grow crops to feed to animals (see pages 20–21). But meat is a good source of protein, and it's important for us to have a balanced diet. So how can we stay healthy whilst buying and eating meat in a way that is kind to the environment? Here are some ideas:

FRUIT AND VEGETABLES
One way to eat less meat is to eat more plants! Choose fruit and vegetables that have been grown locally, or why not grow your own vegetable patch at home or at school? Salad leaves, tomatoes, carrots and potatoes all taste better straight from the garden.

LOCAL MEAT
When you do buy meat, ask your grown-up to look out for food that has been grown locally and raised in a way that does not damage the environment.

MEAT ALTERNATIVES
Buying less meat is a great start – choose one day a week when you try not to eat anything made from animals. Lentils and pulses are a good meat alternative.

BEANS

RED LENTILS

LOCAL MEAT

BETTER BUYING HABITS

Before you buy something, think about these things first:

CAN I BUY IT SECONDHAND?
Things don't have to be brand new to be exciting!

CAN I BUY IT RECYCLED?
Products that are made of recycled materials, such as recycled paper, use resources that would otherwise have been wasted.

IS IT REUSABLE?
Disposable or single-use items, such as paper plates or plastic straws, are only used once and then thrown away. It is much better to buy things that can be used over and over again.

WAS IT MADE LOCALLY?
Buying things that have been made or grown locally makes it easy to trace what impact they have had on the environment. It also means that very little fossil fuels will have been used in transporting them to the shop.

SAY IT LOUD!

USE *your* VOICE

If you told every single person you know about the problems facing forests, and what we can do to help them, how many people do you think that message would reach? Now imagine if every one of those people told every person THEY know the same message. It doesn't take long to spread the message a long way, does it?

Your voice is powerful! No one is too young or too small to make a difference. Many children around the world have used their voices to stand up for what they believe in. Here are some ways that you can use your voice to stand up for forests.

Write to companies

Tell companies that do not act in a responsible way that you think what they are doing is not right. If lots of people send the same message, eventually companies will have to listen.

- Tell them if the ingredients they use are harmful to forests and explain that you will not buy their products until they remove them.

- Ask them to put in place 'zero deforestation' policies. These trace where their products come from and make sure no trees have been cut down to make them.

- Ask them to use as little packaging as possible on their products, and to make it from recycled or biodegradable materials. Ask how to get rid of packaging responsibly.

Help your family!

Help your grown-ups when they are going shopping by reminding them to pick products that are sustainably produced and contain as little packaging as possible. You could be responsible for always making sure the reusable bags are ready, or offer to check labels for sustainable ingredients. Even swapping just one item for a sustainable product will make a big difference.

SPEAK OUT!

Spread the word at school

Does your school have an eco-council? If so, join it. If it doesn't have one, why not start one? Eco-councils can make lots of fantastic changes to the way schools are run. You could:

- Make sure every classroom has recycling bins and a place to store paper and card that can be used again for crafts.

- Remind everyone to turn off lights and electronics when they leave the room.

- Give an assembly about deforestation and how we can help to avoid it.

- Plant trees in the school grounds.

- Have a school fundraiser to raise money for organisations that protect rainforests.

- Start a campaign to make your school palm oil free.

Write to politicians

If you feel strongly about an issue, write to the politicians in charge. This could be a local politician, if it is an issue affecting the area where you live, such as local woodland being cut down. Or it might be the leader of a country far away, where deforestation is a big problem. The more people who use their voices to stand up for forests, the more likely it is that politicians will listen.

TALK!

PUT *it on* PAPER

A letter can be a powerful way to get your message across and make your voice heard. Here are some tips:

- **MAKE YOUR LETTER PERSONAL:** Explain the issues that affect you directly, and why it is so important that something is done about them.

- **BE POLITE:** Your message will be stronger if you write it in a way that is respectful.

- **KNOW THE FACTS:** Your letter will be taken more seriously if you back up your argument with facts.

- **BE HELPFUL:** Suggest the changes that you think need to be made and how they would make a positive difference.

- **DON'T GIVE UP:** If the person you are writing to doesn't reply, or if nothing changes, write again!

BE INSPIRED!

Did you know that there are many careers out there for people who want to help forests? From jobs in science and technology to charity and the arts, there are lots of different ways to make a difference. Which job might you like to choose in the future?

LAWYER
By studying laws and understanding rules, lawyers can help indigenous groups and local people who want to protect their forests. They might work in an office or stand up in court.

INVENTOR
Clever inventors think up brilliant new ideas for protecting our forests. They are great at thinking of new ways to solve old problems.

TEACHER
Explaining the importance of trees and forests to children at school will make sure they grow up wanting to protect them. One day, those children will be the grown-ups that are running the world!

FARMER
We will always need food to eat! Farmers can make sure their crops and animals are farmed in a way that does not harm forests, by planting trees on their land and not clearing forested areas.

ARTIST
Through street art, paintings and art installations, artists can draw attention towards the problems facing forests, and inspire us to act to help them.

ARCHITECT
Tree-friendly architects help to make our cities green by designing houses and spaces that contain lots of trees and other plants.

JOURNALIST

When forests are damaged, journalists make sure that everybody knows the facts by searching for evidence and writing stories about what has happened.

CHARITY WORKER

Hundreds of charities fight against deforestation. There are lots of different jobs within these charities, including fundraising and communications.

FIELD RESEARCHER

Field researchers visit forests to learn more about the amazing animals and plants that live there, so they can be protected.

SCIENTIST

Scientists research why deforestation and climate change are a problem for the world, and help to come up with solutions, such as renewable energy.

WRITER

Like teachers, books can teach people about the importance of trees and forests. They can also give us ideas about how to live planet-friendly lives.

RECYCLING OFFICER

Making sure that all of our waste is disposed of correctly is really important, because lots of it can be used again and made into new things.

FOREST RANGER

Forest rangers patrol our most threatened forests, protecting the plants and animals that live there from harm.

POLITICIAN

People working in the government can help to write rules that protect trees and forested areas.

CONSERVATIONIST

Conservationists help to protect the natural world. Sometimes they work with the government to help them make decisions that are kind to the environment.

GLOSSARY

ATMOSPHERE The mixture of gases that surrounds Earth.

BIODEGRADABLE Something that will eventually decompose after it has been used.

CAMOUFLAGE The body shape, colour or pattern that helps a living thing to hide by matching its surroundings.

CARBON DIOXIDE A gas breathed out by people and animals, which is also produced by burning carbon.

CLIMATE The typical weather conditions in a particular place or area over a number of years.

CLIMATE CHANGE The change in Earth's climate over time. The term is generally used to describe the rise in temperature of Earth's atmosphere, caused by the increase of particular gases, such as carbon dioxide.

CONSERVATION Protecting things found in nature such as wildlife and plants, and keeping the environment clean and healthy.

CONSERVATIONIST Someone who tries to protect the natural world from damage by humans.

DECOMPOSE To break down and decay.

DEFORESTATION The clearing of forest for timber or other uses, for example, farming.

DIVERSITY If something is diverse, it contains lots of different elements.

DRONE A flying robot that is controlled remotely by someone on the ground.

ECOSYSTEM All the living and non-living things found in a particular area.

ECOTOURISM A type of travel to natural areas that has a low impact on the environment, appreciates plants and wildlife, and is respectful to local people.

ENDANGERED At risk of becoming extinct.

ENVIRONMENT The natural world, either in a local area or on the planet as a whole.

EROSION The process by which the surface of something is gradually destroyed and removed.

EVAPORATING Turning from a liquid into a gas, for example, water turning to steam.

EXTINCT No longer existing, having died out as a species.

FOSSIL FUEL A fuel such as oil, coal or gas, which was formed in the Earth a long time ago from the remains of dead plants or animals.

GREENHOUSE GASES Gases in Earth's atmosphere which keep in the planet's heat. Carbon dioxide is one of the greenhouse gases.

HABITAT The place where an animal or plant is normally found.

INDIGENOUS PEOPLE The first people who lived in a place, not people who came to live there later.

LEAF LITTER A layer of dead leaves, twigs and bark that have fallen to the ground.

LOGGING The process of cutting down trees to sell as timber or pulp.

MAMMAL A warm-blooded animal that has a backbone and fur or hair, and produces milk to feed its young.

MIDDLE AGES The period of time between 500 and 1500 CE; also known as the Medieval period.

MIGRATE To travel long distances according to the seasons, usually to find food or a mate.

MINERALS Pure, natural, non-living substances, such as metals, quartz and diamonds.

MINING The process of digging materials out of the ground, such as coal, diamonds and cobalt.

NUTRIENT Substances that living things need in order to survive and grow.

OXYGEN A gas found in the air that is breathed by people and animals, and produced by plants.

PLANTATION A large area of land, usually in the Tropics, where a single crop such as soya beans, palm oil, sugar cane or coffee is grown.

POACHERS People who illegally hunt or trap wild animals.

POLLINATION The process of spreading pollen from one flower to another, so that flowering plants can make seeds.

POLLUTION The addition of dirty or harmful substances to land, air or water.

PROTEIN A nutrient found in meat, fish, eggs, nuts, seeds and beans that is an important part of our diet.

PULPING A chemical process that removes fibres from wood so that it can be made into paper and cardboard.

RAINFOREST A forest in a tropical area that receives a high amount of rainfall.

RECYCLE To re-use something, or to treat something that has already been used so that it can be used again.

RENEWABLE ENERGY A type of energy that does not get used up, for example energy made by the wind, water or Sun.

SILT Soil or sand that's carried along in a river and then later sinks.

SPECIES A group of animals or plants that are similar and able to breed with each other.

SUSTAINABLE To use things in a way that means they will still be there in the future and not used up.

SWAMP A type of wetland covered with trees.

TAIGA FOREST A forest in the cold, northern region of the world, made up of mostly evergreen trees.

TEMPERATE Having temperatures that are very mild (never very hot or very cold). Temperate forests grow north and south of the Tropics.

TEMPERATE DECIDUOUS FOREST A temperate forest made up of deciduous trees, which lose their leaves in the autumn.

TROPICAL Coming from, found in or typical of the Tropics – the area just above and below the Equator.

WATER CYCLE The circular journey that water takes as it moves around Earth. It evaporates from oceans, rivers and land, cools and condenses into clouds, and then falls to Earth again as rain or snow.

First published in the UK in 2020 by

Ivy Kids

An imprint of The Quarto Group
The Old Brewery
6 Blundell Street
London N7 9BH
United Kingdom
www.QuartoKnows.com

British Library Cataloguing-in-Publication Data

A catalogue record for this book is available from the British Library.

ISBN: 978-1-78240-951-9

This book was conceived, designed & produced by

Ivy Kids

58 West Street, Brighton BN1 2RA, United Kingdom

PUBLISHER   Georgia Amson-Bradshaw
MANAGING EDITOR   Susie Behar
COMMISSIONING EDITOR   Hannah Dove
ART DIRECTOR   Kate Haynes & Hanri van Wyk
IN-HOUSE EDITOR   Lucy Menzies
EXTERNAL EDITOR   Claire Saunders
EXTERNAL DESIGNER   Suzie Harrison

Manufactured in Guangdong, China EB072020

1 3 5 7 9 10 8 6 4 2